CHICKEN SOUP FOR THE SOUL® CELEBRATES GRANDMOTHERS

CHICKEN SOUP FOR THE SOUL® CELEBRATES GRANDMOTHERS

A Collection in Words and Photographs by
Jack Canfield and Mark Victor Hansen
and
Lori Brystan

Health Communications, Inc.
Deerfield Beach, Florida

www.hcibooks.com
www.chickensoup.com

Subject matter, locality and/or people in the photographs may not be the actual locality or people in the stories. Names of certain individuals have been changed to protect their identity.

Library of Congress Cataloging-in-Publication Data

Chicken soup for the soul celebrates grandmothers : a collection in words and photographs / [compiled] by Jack Canfield and Mark Victor Hansen and Lori Brystan.
    p. cm.
ISBN 0-7573-0249-1

    1. Grandmothers—Anecdotes.   2. Grandparent and child—Anecdotes.   I. Canfield, Jack, 1944–   II. Hansen, Mark Victor.   III. Brystan, Lori.

HQ759.9.C53 2005
306.874'5—dc22

2004060787

Publisher: Health Communications, Inc.
                3201 S.W. 15th Street
                Deerfield Beach, FL 33442-8190

Cover design by Larissa Hise Henoch
Inside formatting by Dawn Von Strolley Grove

CONTENTS

hen a child is born, so are grandmothers.

—Judith Levy

CRINKLES AND CROW'S FEET

I gasped in horror as I stared at the picture on my new driver's license. "Who is that old woman?" I cried, clapping my hand over my eyes. What happened to the slender, blonde girl who used to be there? I peeked out between my fingers. With just the barest hint of a smile curving her lips, the unfamiliar face gazed steadily back at me. There were crow's feet crinkling out from her eyes and multiple strands of gray streaking through her hair. Though I didn't recognize her face, my name marched boldly across the bottom of the license. I shuddered and tucked the offensive piece of plastic into my pocketbook.

For the next few days I walked around in a state of mild shock. Physically, I didn't feel a bit older. In fact, I felt as chipper and cheerful as always. But I hadn't seen a picture of myself in a long time, and the license photo was a rude awakening. The only good thing about it, I told myself, was that nobody else who saw it seemed shocked by my mature appearance. Maybe I was the only one surprised by the fact that age had snuck up behind me and unkindly retouched my looks.

I fought to get past the nagging plastic reminder that I would never be smooth-faced or blithely young again. No matter how I struggled, I found myself swinging between bouts of depression because I looked so old and pride that I had thus far survived all the curve balls life had thrown my way.

Then, while browsing through the newspaper one day, I spotted something that grabbed my attention. I pulled the paper closer and squinted at the grainy black-and-white photograph of a former classmate. I added up how long it had been since we had graduated from high school. Frowning in disbelief, I counted again. How could it be possible that thirty years had zipped by? I studied his face. Though he had aged well, there was no doubt he hadn't seen eighteen in a very long time. With a sigh, I realized that all the people I remembered as young and baby-faced were now older and life-worn. Besides, many were grandparents. I consoled myself with the fact that at least I wasn't *that* far gone.

Then the telephone rang. It was my daughter, calling from work. "Are you sitting down?" she asked.

"Yes," I said, an uneasy knot twisting in my stomach. In my experience, conversations that started like this never brought good news.

"I'm pregnant!" she blurted out.

Instantly, myriad emotions washed over me—shock, fear, concern for my insulin-dependent daughter and a blinding, bright burst of extreme joy. Laura's voice sounded from the receiver, "Mom? Are you happy?"

"Oh, yes!" I replied.

Suddenly, the idea of being a grandmother seemed pretty wonderful as I fell totally and completely in love with the idea of the baby-to-be. My hands itched to start crocheting, and before the week was out, a blanket, two pairs of tiny booties and a soft little cap emerged from my flying crochet hook. With a heart full of prayers for the health and safety of my daughter and her unborn baby, I spent my days planning the fun things I would do with the new little one and my nights worrying myself sick thinking about all the things that could go wrong.

Finally the tense months of waiting were over, and on one of the coldest, nastiest days of the year, Bailey made his grand entrance into the world. At nearly ten pounds, he was the largest newborn I had ever seen. And he was perfect!

Later, as I proudly displayed his picture, a few friends and relatives teased me about my updated status. "Old Grandma," one of them snickered.

"You're just jealous," I retorted. Yes, I was a grandma and darned happy about it. I treasured every moment I spent cuddling that sweet little bundle.

One day while visiting, I gave Bailey a loud smooch on the cheek, and he rewarded me with a toothless grin. As he stared up into my face, he squinted his eyes and giggled.

"Look, Mom!" cried Laura. "When he laughs, his eyes crinkle up like yours do."

What? My eyes crinkle when I laugh? I sat back in amazement. Suddenly it dawned on me that my crow's feet had emerged from years of smiles and laughter. And if Bailey crinkled his eyes when he smiled, that meant someday he'd have crow's feet, too. I burst into peals of joyful laughter, not caring how many lines spread across my face. Somehow, crinkles and crow's feet never sounded so good.

Anne Culbreath Watkins

Just about the time a woman thinks her work is done, she becomes a grandmother.

—E. H. Dreschnack

A grandmother pretends she doesn't know who you are on Halloween.

—Erma Bombeck

A GIANT LEAP FOR GRANDMA

"Watch me, watch me, Grandma!" Sam pleaded with an eight-year-old's urgency. And despite the pulls of two other grandsons equally bent on seizing my attention, I managed to go outside and watch Sam climb onto the trampoline in his backyard.

The trampoline is now Sam's passion. He dashes out to jump on it the minute he gets home from school, barely pausing for his usual after-school snack. And he's on that trampoline until darkness sets in.

As requested, I watched my redheaded, little fireball of a grandson perform his leaps, lunges and new tricks. I alternately hid my eyes in terror and cheered for Sam, whose courage made my cowardice all the more striking.

I have never been brave. I used to blame it on the culture in which I came of age, one in which girls were not encouraged to be athletic. I certainly recall the hideous gym suits we wore, complete with puffy bloomers, and how notions of girls playing hockey or lacrosse were nonexistent. Instead, we did calisthenics several times a week and were told to "Keep your figures lovely, girls."

For all of my life, I've shied away from sports, partly from intimidation and partly from disinterest. It's hard to love what you've never known.

But watching Sam on the trampoline on the kind of brilliantly sunny, cool day when anything seems possible made me feel a stab of envy for this grandson's marvelous ease with his body and his pride in testing it.

And then Sam tossed out the invitation he has so often:

"Grandma, come on the trampoline with me." My instant reaction was to shrug off the offer with a joke. "Now can you imagine Grandma on that thing? I'm way too old. . . ."

But this time, Sam persisted. And this time, my defenses crumbled.

Maybe it was the weather or Sam's delightful earnestness or the realization that life is short—and getting shorter every day. And maybe, just maybe, I could master a jump or two.

Step one was, literally, a step. I had to get onto the trampoline that suddenly seemed impossible to ascend. But with Sam as my trusty guide, I managed to climb aboard. And just that much seemed a remarkable leap of faith for a self-confessed wimp.

Elated, Sam became my gentle, patient teacher. Even as I insisted that I was getting off, that this thing was way too dangerous for the likes of me, my eight-year-old cheerleader spurred me on. "Just try one jump!" Sam begged. "You won't fall. I promise."

And those blue eyes looked at me so imploringly that I somehow screwed up my almost nonexistent spunk and literally took the leap. Into the air my body went for a split second, and oh my, it was glorious. I think I shrieked in both delight and relief that I had crossed this physical boundary.

I landed safely and in time to see Sam absolutely beaming. The "I told you so" went unspoken, but it was palpable nonetheless.

I'd love to say that I spent the rest of the day perfecting my trampoline form, but that would be fudging. I did execute a couple more jumps to the delightful sound of Sam's cheers and hoots of joy. And I did try to memorize the feeling of pure exhilaration and freedom as I let my legs take me on this new journey. But I was far too prudent to test the limits of this unlimber body, whatever the spirit yearned to prove.

Sam was disappointed when I retreated back inside, promising to watch his antics from the kitchen window. But I honestly felt a new spring in my step as I walked away from my testing ground. And I could swear that I'd grown an inch or two.

As with so many glorious moments in life, this one was unplanned and surely unexpected. And that made it all the richer. Suddenly, I was a grandmother who had jumped on a trampoline. I had freed some ancient sense of limits, some long-buried insecurities.

And with any luck, I'll be back on that trampoline before long, jumping higher and higher in both real and metaphoric terms.

Sally Friedman

ew things are more delightful than grandchildren fighting over your lap.

—Doug Larson

Being a preacher's kid is never easy, so I was understandably thrilled when Dad decided to hang up his reverend's collar, move to a new town and head for a new life in the corporate world. Most ten-year-olds would be upset to pack up and move away, but I would have gladly hitchhiked out of town just to get away from being the "son of the preacher."

Early in the summer we packed up our furniture, clothes and Grandma Schaal and headed off to Grapevine, Texas. Grapevine is a small town, a suburb of the suburbs of Dallas. The most attractive part of the area is the large lake that shares a name with the town. In nervous anticipation, we drove into the trailer park and pulled up to our new home. It would be crowded with the six of us plus Grandma living in a singlewide, three-bedroom house on wheels—but at least it wasn't the parsonage.

A few days after we arrived in Grapevine, my older brother and sisters and my parents all headed off to new jobs in the big city. As the youngest, I had to stay home with Grandma. The summer didn't look promising. Sure, Grandma was active for an eighty-year-old, but what could she do that would interest me? That morning I helped her clean up the house and wash the breakfast dishes. When we were finished she mumbled something about an old fishing rod and then pulled a baseball cap over her thin, unruly white hair. With her simple statement, "We're going fishin'," we were off. We marched down the quiet road and quickly covered the mile-long walk to the lake. And, with a couple of old rods and reels, a few hooks and some stale cheese, we fished.

Every weekday we rushed through the chores and then headed

to the lake. We worked the shoreline with a vengeance. Not being one to waste money on fancy fishing lures or live bait, Grandma demanded that we find creative ways to use what we had. We used a lot of corn, bread and cheese. One time I discovered a nearly dead fish floating listlessly in a shallow, reedy area near the shore. I gingerly scooped it up and gave it to Grandma who, to my surprise and sudden queasiness, proceeded to cut it up and use the guts for bait.

Every day was an adventure. We kept trying to find better spots or come up with different approaches. One time, a guy fishing near us had caught a whole pail of catfish, which he offered to us free. I couldn't believe our good fortune. This became a promising trend as we worked the area near the boat launch. Fishermen, seeing us empty-handed, would often kindly offer us some of their catch.

We fished and fished and fished that entire summer. We tried it all—and we never caught a thing.

It was a summer I will never forget. What I had thought would be a time of loneliness and boredom instead turned into a time of fun, adventure and discovery. I'm still not sure what drew Grandma to that lake every day. She wasn't one to talk a lot or share her feelings. Maybe she felt young again as she cast her line out into the water. It could be she stood there remembering times with Grandpa. Maybe she was just trying to help out her lonely grandson.

Summer went by quickly and school began. I made new friends, and my life moved forward. Grandma and I never went fishing again.

I soon grew into a busy teenager and before long graduated from high school. Grandma eventually moved back East to live with some of her other children, while I got married and had kids of my own.

A few years ago, in her nineties, Grandma passed away. Her

funeral was thousands of miles away from where I live, and I was unable to attend. In a way, it was a good thing that I never saw her in a casket. When I think of Grandma Schaal, I always picture her standing by the lake, fishing.

As I rush through life in the big city, I often remember that summer by the lake. It usually makes me want to spend a little more time with my kids, and it always makes me want to go fishing. One day, when my turn comes to pass on to the next life, I'm going to march into heaven, grab the first fishing rod I find and start looking for Grandma. She won't be hard to find. She'll be wearing an old baseball cap and standing beside a lake with her line in the water. This time she'll be catching fish.

Daniel Favor

A grandmother holds her grand-children's hands for a while; their hearts forever.

—Unknown

STICKY MEMORIES

It was a warm summer day, and my kids were driving me crazy. They were licking Popsicles and traipsing back and forth between the patio and our family room. With each trip, they left behind a sticky display of fingerprints on our large sliding glass door.

"Watch what you're doing! Keep your fingers off the glass!" I yelled at them. Granted, our sliding door was a real bear. The track had warped from the weight of the heavy glass. The only way to get the door open was to grab the handle with one hand, prop your foot against the wall for leverage and pull with all your might. At three years old, my daughter Kelly had very little "might." She would try to open the door by running her fingers across the glass. Her older brother, Derrick, was a bit stronger, but even he soon tired of the effort. When he wanted back in, he would pound on the door with his fists.

My mother happened to be visiting and noted my temper flaring.

"Don't be so hard on them," she admonished. "Some day you will miss those little fingerprints on the glass."

"Oh, right," I replied, as I headed for the closet where I kept the window cleaner.

"Well, your grandmother sure was fond of *your* fingerprints on the glass of her French doors," my mom said, as she opened the door for her granddaughter.

"What are you talking about? Grandmother was a fastidious housekeeper. She wouldn't even let us play in her living room. We were relegated to the guest room or the attic!" Not that my sister or I minded our restrictions. The attic was filled with trunks full of treasures: long evening gowns for dress up, old teddy bears and wooden soldiers. Best of all, we could spy on unsuspecting adults by peering through the attic fan's grating.

We only saw my mother's family for a few weeks each summer. They lived in Arkansas, and we called California home. Those summers were a magical time of picnicking at the lake and chasing lightning bugs with our cousins.

Now, as hard as I tried, I could not dredge up a single memory related to fingerprints on my grandmother's French doors. I remembered the doors well. They stood in the formal dining room, and after supper we exited through them to rejoin our friends at play.

"I would offer to clean the windows," my mother continued. "But Mother wouldn't let me. 'Those little fingerprints are all I have to remind me of the girls when they leave,' she would say."

If there were tears at the time of our departure, we never saw them. It was only after hearing my mother's story that I realized the intensity of my grandmother's love. Only now, as a mother, could I comprehend her longing to hold on to a little piece of us.

It's been years since that summer day when I fumed over my children's fingerprints. Derrick and Kelly are grown now. French doors that open easily have replaced that troublesome sliding door.

"Nana, come outside and watch me shoot baskets?" Aaron yells from the patio, as he pounds on the doors to get my attention.

On the other side of the French doors, Trevor toddles on chubby legs. As he presses his face against the glass to get a better glimpse of his big brother, I swoop him into my arms. Noting the tiny fingerprints left behind, I feel a lump in my throat.

My son and his wife have decided to trade their California residency for Colorado. They are packing up their house, and in two weeks they will be gone. I know the boys will love their new

Rocky Mountain home—so many lakes to picnic by and lots of cousins to join in the chase for fireflies.

We will keep in touch, of course. They will come back to visit. And until then, I have their fingerprints to cherish.

Mary Ann Cook

A mother becomes a true grandmother the day she stops noticing the terrible things her children do because she is so enchanted with the wonderful things her grandchildren do.

—Lois Wyse

randmas are just antique little girls.

—G. W. Curtis

JENNY'S ANTIQUE

My six-year-old granddaughter stares at me as if seeing me for the first time. "Grandma, you are an antique," she says. "You are old. Antiques are old. You are my antique."

I am not satisfied to let the matter rest there. I take out *Webster's Dictionary* and read the definition to Jenny. I explain, "An antique is not just old, it's an object existing since or belonging to earlier times, a work of art, a piece of furniture."

"Antiques are treasured," I tell Jenny as I put away the dictionary. "They have to be handled carefully because sometimes they are very valuable. To qualify as an antique, the object has to be at least one hundred years old.

"I'm only sixty-seven," I remind Jenny.

We look around the house for antiques. There is a bureau that was handed down from one aunt to another and finally to me. "It's very old," I tell her. "I try to keep it polished, and I show it off whenever I can. You do that with antiques." When Jenny gets older and understands such things, I might also tell her that whenever I look at the bureau or touch it, I am reminded of the aunt so dear to me who gave it to me as a gift. I see her face, though she is no longer with us. I even hear her voice and recall her smile. I remember myself as a little girl leaning against this antique, listening to one of her stories. The bureau does that for me.

There is a picture on the wall purchased at a garage sale. It is dated 1867. "Now, that's an antique," I boast. "Over one hundred years old." It is marked up and scratched and not in very good condition. "Sometimes age does that," I tell Jenny, "but the marks are good marks. They show living, having been around. That's something to display with pride. In fact, sometimes the more an object shows age, the more valuable it can become." It is important that I believe this for my own self-esteem.

Our tour of antiques continues. There is a large vase on the floor. It has been in my house for a long time. I'm not certain where it came from, but I didn't buy it new. Then there's the four-poster bed, sent to me forty years ago by an uncle who had slept in it himself for fifty years.

"One thing about antiques," I explain to Jenny, "is that they usually have a story. They've been in one home and then another, handed down from one family to another, traveling all over the place. They've lasted through years and years. They could have been tossed away or ignored or destroyed or lost. But instead, they survived."

For a moment Jenny looks thoughtful. "I don't have any antiques but you," she says. Then her face brightens. "Could I take you to school for show and tell?"

"Only if I fit into your backpack," I answer.

And then Jenny's antique lifts her up and embraces her in a hug that will last through the years.

Harriet May Savitz

MAKE A MEMORY

"Are you and the kids going to be home this weekend?" I asked my son. "I want to come up and see you guys."

"We'll be home. When can you get here?"

"I found an affordable flight on the Internet. I'll be there in three days."

"Cool. I'll tell the kids."

"I want to do something fun. Let's make Christmas cookies—the kind we used to make when you were a kid, the cutout ones that you decorate with icing and colored sugars."

"Yeah, I like those. And the boys will, too."

It would be a messy, fun, memory-filled weekend. Since every moment I spend with my grandchildren is precious, I didn't want to waste time going to the grocery store once I arrived at their house. Nor did I want to bend over a mixing bowl when I could be holding a child in my arms. So I made the dough and the frosting ahead of time. After mixing up the dough, I placed it in an airtight container. Then I made a butter frosting, licking the bowl and the beaters afterward, just like I did when I was a young mom, raising two sons. Oh, what memories!

After pouring the frosting into another container, and putting both in the fridge, I gathered the colored sugars for decorating. Of course we'd need green and red, but how about blue, yellow, pink and purple? It was our tradition, when my boys were small, to add chocolate sprinkles and to use Red Hots for the tips of the trees and the reindeer noses.

With everything packed and ready, I rolled two suitcases into the airport terminal that Friday morning. The larger one held all the presents to put under the tree, and the other held the rolling pin, cookie cutters, and the dough and frosting containers nestled in ice packs for the trip.

Saturday morning found a house full of kids gathered around the kitchen table. My brother and his children had joined us for the festivities.

"Grandma, can I roll out the dough?" asked nine-year-old Nick.

"I want to make a reindeer," said little five-year-old Cole.

The first few attempts produced Santas that stuck to the floured table and reindeer with only two legs. We kept on going, though, and finally got the hang of it. Some of the kids wanted to throw back the cookies that were misshapen and less than perfect, but we kept every one. It was fun after they were baked to see the elongated star and the funny-looking stocking. After all, it's part of Christmas to accept things just the way they are.

We rolled out the dough many times and cut out stockings,

trees, Santas, reindeer, stars and bells. While we cut out more, we put the first two trays of cookies into the oven. We finished baking the last batch two hours later. We had over four dozen cookies to frost and decorate.

Out came the box from my suitcase with sugars in all shades of the rainbow. We put them in separate bowls, all lined up on one side of the table. The adults frosted the cookies before handing them to a waiting child, who would walk along the row of colors and sprinkle a little bit of red, a touch of yellow, and maybe a dash of green.

"I want a stocking, Grandma!" little Cole yelled out.

"I want a star," Amanda demanded. And on it went, the adults barely keeping up with the eager children.

As tray after tray was filled with brightly colored cookies, we oohed and aahed over each one. "Look at mine, Grandma!" shouted Nick. "I put extra frosting on it; see the hump?"

"Look at my bell, Daddy," said Kayla, "it has a Red Hot right at the top."

I thought about the memories we had all just made as I watched my son and his uncle wipe off the table, put all the colored sugar away and grab the vacuum to clean up the floor. Happy memories. Loving memories. Fun times shared with laughter and joy.

"Who made the star with all the different colored points?" "Who made this one with the pretty stripes down the side?" "Nick, is this one yours with the extra frosting on it?" "Can I eat it?"

The afternoon wore into evening, and cookie after cookie disappeared from the trays. Little hands would reach up and choose just the colors they were looking for. It was a happy day. But the best part came as music to my ears when I heard, "Grandma, can we do this again next year?"

B. J. Taylor

Grandmas are moms with lots of frosting.

—Unknown

WHAT'S IN A NAME?

I am a grandma by default. Excuse me, I need to rephrase that—I am a *step*-grandma by default. I am part of a grandparenting unit I entered by means of marriage to my widowed boyfriend.

If your reaction is that I am being a slave to semantics, then you most likely are not involved in a blended family. Those of us who are know that semantics is either the path of diplomacy or the route to familial brouhaha.

When I began dating Bob, his middle child was expecting her first child—Bob's first grandchild. Jill and her husband lived far away, clear across the country. I first met Jill and her beautiful baby girl when they came home for a visit. Kelly was only three months old. By the time Bob and I married two years later, Kelly was beginning to talk. She called me Patty.

Shortly after our wedding, a second grandchild, Ryan, came along. If one baby can steal your heart, two will hold your entire mind, body and soul captive.

But while my heart longed to smother these gorgeous children with love, I was more than a little hesitant to insert myself into the role of grandma when I felt I had no claim to the name.

I took my concerns to my husband, asking him how I should engage the grandchildren without overstepping any boundaries. I didn't want to be separated from the love or the involvement of each stage of their growth simply because I was not a charter member of the family. And I definitely did not want to be viewed as disinterested, when in fact I felt deeply invested.

I told Bob I yearned for the luxury of casual acceptance—the kind where you can lavish blatant, biased praise over the smallest achievements without looking like you're pandering or step in with the sage advice of years and experience without appearing like a know-it-all. I coveted the safety net of ownership.

Bob's wisdom came in the form of a parable. He told me a lovely story about his paternal step-grandfather, Guy. Bob's dad lost his own father when he was only fourteen years old. Bob's grandmother, Gigi, married Guy a few years later. Bob's eyes glistened with childlike anticipation when he spoke of Guy and Gigi. They had owned an ice cream store. (Who among us would not wish for our grandparents to own an ice cream store?)

Beyond spooning dollops of ice cream into Bob's eager mouth, Guy took Bob fishing. Guy baited and hooked not only the fish, but young Bob, too. Guy reeled Bob in with his kind, gentle and loving spirit. They laughed, joked and did "guy" things. The only name Guy ever held was Guy, but Bob's heart still speaks *Grandpa* thirty years after Guy's death.

Bob's story was very comforting to me. I know that gaining

acceptance as a new step-grandparent can take time. I can wait. In the meantime, my love pours out into their open, willing spirits in spurts, sometimes gushing forth, other times more measured, but always genuine and pure.

When the time comes, and in my best grandma fashion—as all good grandmas do—I will relate a multitude of family stories to Kelly and Ryan and the nameless wonders of future step-grandchildren and grandchildren. My wish is that all the "grands" will be cousins-in-arms, gathered around the sprightly little old woman (me) while she weaves her tales.

And the first story I will tell will be this: One day not so long ago, in a city far away, four-year-old Kelly was happily chatting to her mom when her mother mentioned something about Grandpa. Kelly asked for clarification: "My grandpa with grandma, or my grandpa with my *Patty*?"

At this point in the storytelling I will pause to ask, "How do you like that? I am *Kelly's Patty!*" I will shout these words with tremendous animation, flinging my arms wide open as if to embrace the world, throwing my head back, giggling in delight, kicking my bare feet into the air and wiggling my toes. I will proclaim to all the children of the generation two steps down from mine that the possessive "my," followed by whatever name that comes to mind, creates a glorious state of being.

Patty Swyden Sullivan

f nothing is going well, call your grandmother.

—Italian Proveb

MY FIVE-DOLLAR FRIENDS

They sat on the sofa hugging each other, legs entwined in a fun embrace—two happy faces looking toward the camera. Although fifty years separate them in age, never were two hearts closer. Somewhere in my mind, I wondered how two people, who lived halfway around the world from each other for so long, could end up caring for each other as these two did.

I took down the heart-shaped crystal frame from the top shelf and dusted the glass, thinking an appropriate title might read "Five-Dollar Friends." If you look straight at the photo, the grandmother is the "five-dollar friend" on the right. Dressed in a light blue, polyester pantsuit and sporting a white crown of glory on her head, she reflects all the goodness any grandma could hope to possess. On the left, and wrapped in her arms, is the college-age granddaughter: socks, no shoes, faded jeans and somebody's old soccer shirt.

Both grandmother and granddaughter have very limited incomes. One lives in a retirement village in central Florida, and the other has been putting herself through school for the last six years. Usually, for both of them, the money runs out before the end of the month arrives. So it was that, several years ago, the grandmother lovingly folded a five-dollar bill in an envelope and sent it along to the granddaughter. In so doing, she attached a little note saying, "Just thinking of you, Honey. Hope you can use the money." The granddaughter opened the letter a few days later, and being completely out of money herself, felt as though a hundred-dollar bill had just fallen into her lap. *Girl, go buy yourself a cup of hot coffee!* She smiled as she rushed out the door to her next class.

A few months went by, and the granddaughter felt a tug on her heart to stretch her own budget to the limit. She folded a five-dollar bill, slipped it into a card and sent it on its way to Florida. On her note, just under her name, she wrote the following postscript: "Buy yourself five extra bingo cards this week. And remember, I love you!"

So back and forth the five-dollar bills have traveled over the years. And back and forth the love has grown between these two best friends—one thinking of the other, secret money shipped in the night, love notes dashed on handmade cards.

On one peaceful spring morning the phone rang in Florida. Grandma picked up the receiver, answering with her sing-songy "Yell-O," to which there was no reply. She waited a few seconds and was about to hang up when over the "airwaves" came the smooth, romantic voice of Dean Martin, serenading her on the other end of the line. The orchestra was from the Big Band era, the sound track was from the movie *Swingers* and the phone call was from the granddaughter.

The grandmother didn't miss a beat. While Dean crooned away

on his sentimental words, "You're nobody 'til somebody loves you," her shag carpet was transformed into a checkered dance floor. Holding the portable phone tightly to her ear, she danced to the song in its entirety, only breaking her step when she heard the final note. Then the two girls laughed as they shared their mutual admiration of swing music. The granddaughter told the grandmother that she was just thinking of her as she was painting in her studio, and the grandmother told the granddaughter that she had just mailed her a pair of fluffy leopard house slippers.

Although fifty years separate them in age, never were two hearts closer. And Dean hit it on the money when he sang, "You may be king, you may possess the world and its gold, but gold won't buy you happiness when you're growing old. The world is still the same, you'll never change it, as sure as the stars shine above. You're nobody 'til somebody loves you . . . so find yourself somebody to love."

Charlotte A. Lanham

I can remember what flavor of ice cream cone my grandmother and I shared at Disneyworld; but most of the time, I can't remember what day it is. I guess it depends on what you think is important.

—Katherine, age 13

Grandmothers are a special gift to children.

—G. W. Curtis

A grandmother is a little bit parent, a little bit teacher and a little bit best friend.

—G. W. Curtis

THE BLESSING OF GIVING

Eight-year-old Mary Kathryn was ecstatic as she entered our house. A report card for the past nine weeks was in her hand. "Look, Granddaddy, there is an A in every subject," she excitedly proclaimed. That meant a dollar that he had promised to give her for each A she received.

Sure enough, with a grateful heart for the excellent grades displayed before him, Granddaddy reached in his billfold and counted out six dollars for six As. With a bounce in her step and joy on her face, Mary Kathryn retreated to her room with the money.

These were her riches to spend as she chose!

I prayed she would spend it wisely, and I delighted in watching her little mind spin trying to decide how to use it.

A couple of days later, Mary Kathryn asked me to take her to a dollar store. "Grandma, I want to spend four of my six dollars to replace the items in our treat box at school. That will leave two dollars for me," was her plea to me. That pleased me very much, and I hastily made arrangements to go.

Picking out just four things at the dollar store wasn't easy. She loved it all! After depositing some items in our basket, she found herself vacillating. She rearranged everything in the basket several times. Finally she had it narrowed down to six items. Exactly the amount of money her granddaddy had given her for the exemplary report card.

"Help me choose four things, Grandma," Mary Kathryn pleaded.

Wanting the decision to be hers, I gave her all the time she needed. It was a perplexing position for an eight-year-old. There were six treats she really wanted to share with the other children at school. But she only had four dollars to spend if she kept two for herself. She already had those two items picked out and placed on one side of the basket.

Silently, I said a short prayer for her.

Suddenly, her eyes lit up! I knew she had decided what she was going to do. My sweet Mary Kathryn, with the kind, sensitive spirit, said, "I know, Grandma. I will use all of my six dollars to give to the treat box at school." My heart melted right there.

All the while I thought she was struggling in her mind to come up with the right toys for her dollars, Mary Kathryn was using her *heart* to solve the problem. She would give it all. And that was the appropriate answer! As her grandma, I sometimes make simple principles unnecessarily complicated. And yet it seemed so obvious to this young child who already understood that it truly is more joyous to give than to receive.

My granddaughter reminded me that day of a lesson on giving that will forever be etched in my memory.

Melva Cooper

OF SATIN AND CEREMONIES

She slips the wedding gown from its padded hanger and fingers the flowing length of pearly satin. She smoothes its streaming folds, lifts its cascading train, tests its lush weight.

Her two daughters had always shared. They shared Barbies and boyfriends, messy bedrooms and midnight secrets, cramp complaints and crowded closets, and finally, a confining college apartment. They even shared the same taste in shoes and clothes. So it came as no surprise when her girls expressed an identical choice in bridal attire: simple, yet elegant. And this gown was both. Luxuriant and luminous. A gown to share—and much too lovely to be packed away forever.

A single shaft of sunlight haloes the fabric with the patina of platinum. It looks fresh and radiant. Radiant the way each of her daughters, in turn, had looked in the custom-designed gown. First the older, then later—rescuing it from the garment bag hanging in a dark closet—the younger. Draped in ivory dreams, brides full of promise and brimming with hope, they stood next to their husbands in solemn ceremonies sealing upon them blessings and new names, celebrating their futures.

That was then. Cleaned and bagged, the dress was once more relegated to a corner in the closet—until now.

One of the girls was asking about the gown. The dress belongs to each girl . . . and yet to both. What else can she do but divide it? What better opportunity for them to share it once again? After all, there's a lavish expanse of the rich fabric.

Spreading the skirt wide, she picks up her sewing scissors in one hand and opens a seam from bodice to hem. And another seam. And yet another. She separates the thread attaching the bustle, removes the train, and snips off the row of covered buttons.

She smiles as she smoothes the pieces. It's time to transform the milky satin into different gowns for a different generation. The old gives birth to the new; it deserves a future. From sections of the bridal skirt and train, she will fashion infant christening gowns. One for each of her daughters to own.

A legacy to share. Gifts from mother to daughters to grand-children and beyond.

The gowns will be simple, yet elegant of course, and fasten with the small salvaged buttons. Talcum soft, the lustrous satin will soon swaddle precious babies held by their fathers during solemn ceremonies—sealing upon them blessings and new names. Grandbabies full of promise and brimming with hope.

She fingers the fabric and straightens the separate sections. She will sew christening gowns to pass down and bond succeeding generations, cherished heirloom gowns to celebrate and share the future . . . with the same passion as the past.

Carol McAdoo Rehme

REALLY ALIVE

Jake asks, "I know what it is like to see, and I know what it is like to breathe, but what is it like to be alive?" Jake is five years old and asks a question that I, his grandmother and sixty-five years older, find difficult to answer.

Yet, I will try, dear Grandson, to answer your question as best I can. But first you must know that it is my answer, and you must find your own. For the response is as individual as a fingerprint. At your age, I thought being alive—really alive—meant something new happened every day: learning something new in school, or discovering something new as soon as I walked outside my home—or even within it. Life meant discovery. Discovery meant life.

And now, Jake, I must admit to you that, after these many years of living, I find being really alive has not changed very much for me. Only, at this time of my life, it is less about discovery of the world around me and more about discovery of myself. Each day that I awaken, I must look within to bring life to my day. Even on the days when it is quiet inside me and there seems little to unearth. Even on the days when I think discovery is only for the young.

Sometimes it is a simple thing that gets me going. Just feeding the pets makes me feel alive. They stand in line each morning, hungry, loving, needing me. They need me every day. They let me know in many ways: a tail wagging, a soft cat paw rubbing my nose, a bird chirping a morning song. I am important to their survival. I am a *somebody.* I am not only a senior citizen, as some refer to me. I am not an old lady as some might see me. I am not just a potential client for assisted living or a consumer of life-extending medications. My pets look upon me as their ageless companion. I am not too old for them, just as you, Jake, are not too young.

You are right, Jake. You are breathing. You are seeing. You are even hearing. But being alive, really alive, is another matter entirely. That is something you have to do yourself. And so do I, even more so now. It is up to me to be sensitive to the world around me, to contribute to its progress. I must have more determination to survive than ever before. It is easy to sit and watch television and nap in a chair. Too easy to wait for others to start my day and convince myself that is the way it should be at this time in my life. But being really alive is my responsibility, Jake, and if I do not take it seriously, I might just be here, existing. And that is not enough.

Giving makes me feel alive. I feel things churn inside me when I give. I feel an energy seep into these sometimes tired bones. I feel a connection to the rest of the world when I share, and that makes me feel alive. I crochet afghans and give them away. I stitch in my feelings and imagine my loved ones using them, curling up peacefully and sweeping the afghans around themselves. I feel alive when I crochet. Do you feel the same way when you color a picture for me to hang on my refrigerator door?

I have a friend who reads to students in school. He is a volunteer. He sits in the middle of a room with children all around him, and he reads them a story. And then they talk about it. Sometimes he tells them stories about himself. He is seventy-four, and he has collected many stories. "I feel so alive," he tells me upon his return from the school. I guess you might feel the same way, Jake, as you learn to read.

Another retired man I know says he starts each day with a shower. "I dress as if I'm going to work. Whether I'm going out or not, whether I'm going to see anyone else or be by myself, I put on a fresh shirt and pressed trousers. Then I'm ready to start my day." He takes pride in his personal appearance. I have seen your face, Jake, when you show off your new pair of shoes. It is the same kind of pride.

Sometimes, Jake, I forget that it is up to me to be really alive. I forget there are precious minutes in each day to be used and so many ways to be productive. I ignore the jobs to be done. I forget there are books to read and afghans to create and people to call. Like you, dear Grandson.

And then I dial your number.

"Jake, this is Grandmom," I say. "Tell me, how is your day going?"

And when you tell me about your new dog or the cookies you are eating or the bicycle ride to a friend's house, and when we laugh together while you share your young adventures, I am alive, Jake, and eager to share my adventures with you.

It is very easy to be really alive. Once you know how.

Harriet May Savitz

 t's such a grand thing to be a mother of a mother—that's why the world calls her grandmother.

—Unknown

CONTRIBUTORS

Mary Ann Cook is a humorous speaker and author of *Honey, I'm Home for Good!*. She lives in Escondido, California, where she conducts seminars for retired couples. She enjoys visiting her grandsons, volunteering at nursing homes and working with her daughter's first-grade students. Please contact her at *www.maryanncook.com*.

Melva Cooper is a team writer for Just-A-Minute Devotions and has been published on numerous Web sites and e-zines. She loves NASCAR and is a contributing writer to *Christian Motorsports Illustrated* magazine and a staff writer for *CATCHFENCE.com*. You can read more of her stories at *www.melvacooper.com*.

Daniel Favor is a steelworker in western Canada. He loves working with children and has been involved in various youth ministries for over twenty years. He hopes to soon complete an action-adventure book geared toward young kids. Please contact him at *dwfcaf@telus.net*.

Sally Friedman is a graduate of the University of Pennsylvania, where she majored in English. She has been writing essays since 1975, and her work has appeared in the *New York Times, Ladies' Home Journal, Family Circle* and other national publications. She is the delighted grandmother of seven.

Charlotte A. Lanham is a former columnist and teacher. She is a frequent contributor to *Chicken Soup for the Soul* and writes from her home in Texas. She is cofounder of

Abbi's Room Foundation, a nonprofit organization that provides beds and bedding for children of Habitat for Humanity families. E-mail her at *charlotte.lanham@sbcglobal.net*.

Carol McAdoo Rehme, one of *Chicken Soup*'s managing editors and most prolific contributors, compares grannyhood to homemade happiness—life's natural sweetener. Carol directs a nonprofit, Vintage Voices, Inc., which brings interactive programming to the vulnerable elderly. Speaking engagements and storytelling gigs fill her spare time. Contact her at *carol@rehme.com* or visit *www.rehme.com*.

Harriet May Savitz is the award-winning author of twenty-two books, including *Growing Up At 62* and *Messages From Somewhere: Inspiring Stories Of Life After 60* (Little Treasure Publications) and *More Than Ever—A View From My 70s* (Authors House). To learn more, visit *www.harrietmaysavitz.com* or contact her at *hmaysavitz@aol.com*.

Patty Swyden Sullivan is blessed with an embracing family where bonds are forged through love and understanding. Her stories about family life have been published in anthologies, self-help books and periodicals.

B. J. Taylor loves getting together with her grandsons as often as she can. She is also an animal lover and is writing a book titled *Find Your Dog a Job!* that shows how a dog and its owner can make a difference in their community. B. J. has been published in anthologies, magazines and newspapers and can be reached at *bjtaylor3@earthlink.net*.

Anne Culbreath Watkins is the author of *The Conure Handbook* (Barron's Educational Series, Inc.), as well as scores of nonfiction articles for various magazines, books, newsletters and online venues. She and her husband, Allen, live in Alabama, where they love to spoil their grandchildren, Tyler, Bailey and Chelsea.

PERMISSIONS